PAIDEIA EDUCATION

CHARLOTTE BRONTË

Jane Eyre

Literary analysis

Paideia Education

© Paideia Education, 2020.

ISBN 978-2-7593-0705-0

Legal Deposit: september 2020

Printing Books on Demand GmbH

In de Tarpen 42

22848 Norderstedt, Germany

CONTENTS

- Author's biography.. 9

- Work presentation.. 15

- Summary... 19

- Reasons of success... 33

- Main themes.. 41

- Analysis of the literary movement............................. 47

AUTHOR'S BIOGRAPHY

Charlotte Brontë was born on the 21st of April, 1816, in Thorton, Yorkshire, Great Britain. She was the youngest daughter of Patrick Brontë (a preacher), and of Maria Branwell. Her sisters Maria and Elizabeth were the eldest, Branwell and Emily Jane were the youngest. The Brontë family moved to Haworth where Anne was born in 1820. When Maria Branwell died, aunt Charlotte took care of the household.

The family was quite modest. The four first children started to go to the Cowan Bridge School from 1824 on. Life was hard because of the constant cold and the poor hygiene conditions.

Maria and Elizabeth fell sick and died in a month interval. Charlotte and Emily came back to Haworth and all the children were raised by their aunt. Charlotte found inspiration in Cowan Bridge to describe the Lowood school found in *Jane Eyre*.

The Brontë children often had to take care of themselves, and under Charlotte's tutelage, they all took up to writing. In 1827, they created an imaginary world: the Glass Town confederation. Two imaginary kingdom were invented: Gondal was the invention of Emily and Anne, while Charlotte and Branwell invented Angria. The children also wrote various chronicles, tales, poems, plays and press articles about these kingdoms. These writing activities lasted for years.

In 1831, Charlotte was sent in a boarding school kept by Miss Wooler. It is there that she met Mary Taylor and Ellen Nussey, with whom she remained close for years.

From 1835 to 1845, the Brontë sisters have worked very hard as governesses. Charlotte was apparently a teacher in the second boarding house where she had been sent. She described her teaching experience in *The Professor* and then in *Jane Eyre*.

In 1842, Emily and Charlotte went to Brussels in order to improve their french and german. They also intended to open a school. These motivations pushed them to attend to class in the Héger boarding school where they took up to teaching six months after they had arrived there.

In October, following the death of their aunt Elizabeth branwell, the Brontë sisters went back to Haworth. Charlotte was the only one to go back to the boarding school where the Héger offered her the opportunity to teach english. She fell in love with the Professor Constantin Héger but decided eventually to return permanently to Haworth. She nevertheless had a passionate correspondence with this man she sees as her real mentor, her master. Héger ended this correspondence quite rapidly.

In the end, the Brontë sisters gave up teaching to concentrate on writing.

They first wrote poems that they published themselves under the pseudonym "Bell". As the attempt proved to be a failure, they chose to write novels instead. Under the pseudonyms Currer, Ellis and Acton Bell, they each wrote a novel: *The Professor*, *Wuthering Heights* and *Agnes Grey*. But unlike her two sisters, Charlotte never found a publisher for her novel. Charlotte then wrote Jane Eyre and sent it to the Smith, Elder and Co publishing house, who had previously refused to publish The Professor. Jane Eyre is published in October, 1847 under then name of Currer Bell. It appeared that the success met by Jane Eyre contributed to the publication of Wuthering Heights and of Agnes Grey but these two novels did not have the same success.

Meanwhile, Charlotte had to go through very hard times: Branwell was addicted to gambling, alcohol and opium, and when he got heartbroken, he did not find the strenght to fight tuberculosis and he died in 1848. Emily, who suffered from tuberculosis too, also died three months later. Her sister Anne died in may 1849.

In october 1849, Charlotte's third novel, *Shirley*, was published. *Villette*, that took a year and a half to be written, was published in January 1853. Charlotte renounced working again on the old version of *The Professor*, that got pothumously published thanks to, her friend and biographer, Elizabeth Gaskell.

In 1854, Charlotte married her father's vicar, Arthur Bell Nicholls. She got rapidly pregnant, but being too sick, she died on the 31st of march, 1855.

WORK PRESENTATION

While Charlotte Brontë was trying to get her first novel published (*The Professor*), she also dedicated herself to *Jane Eyre*.

The original title was *Jane Eyre. An autobiography.* She used a male pseudonym and sent the three volumes manuscipt to the Smith, Elder and Co publishing house. The first volume was made of the fifteen first chapters, the second went up to the twentieth chapter and the last one went from the twenty-seventhe to the thirty-eighth chapter.

The first edition was published in October, 16, 1847 and the second one in december. This last one was agremented with a dedication to William Thackeray who was a contemporary author of Charlotte at the time.

The main theme in Jane Eyre is feminine independence, but the novel is also a social critic of the gender roles men and women were to follow at the time. In a more literary angle, *Jane Eyre* is a reflection on the influence of Romanticism and The Gothic on literature.

SUMMARY

Chapter 1

Jane Eyre is a ten years old orphan who lives with her aunt Mrs Reed in the Gateshead estate. She does not get along well with her aunt nor with her cousins John, Eliza and Georgiana. To top it all, the servants tend to ignore her. Being solitary turns her into passionate reader. She is the martyr of her cousin, and when she dares to confront him for the first time, she is punished and taken to the "red room".

Chapter 2

Jane is being moralized by Bessie and Miss Abott before she is left alone. The little girl is sad and hopeless. She is also terrified. Her uncle, Mr Reed died in this very room after he made her wife promise that she would keep the child. Jane is overwhelmed with her imagination and she cries for help to only find her aunt's cruelty. She collapses.

Chapter 3

After this emotional shock, the little girl is looked after, but her aunt deliberately ignores her. Despite all the efforts that Doctor Lloyd makes for Jane to understand how lucky she is to stay in Gateshead, she decides to go to a boarding school.

Chapter 4

Jane spends Christmas and recovery time completely alone. A few days after Christmas, at the request of Mrs Reed, the head of the Lowood school arrives. As a religious devotee, he encourages virtue and humility and blames Jane for her behaviour. Mrs Reed shatters Jane's hopes of a new life in a boarding school. Nevertheless and despite of all this, as soon as the director leaves, she gets mad at her aunt.

Chapter 5

Jane merrily leaves Gateshead and reaches Lowood by stagecoach. She is welcome by Miss Maria Temple, a woman she will get to know afterwards. Jane discovers the boarding school, its rules and its rather humble life conditions. Talking with another pupil allows Jane to know more about the institution and the teachers.

Chapter 6

Jane gets to meet Helen Burns. Helen is a pious and devoted child who is obsessed with improving herself, but she is also the victim of Miss Scatcherd's unfair punishments. Helen is patient and soft. She encourages Jane to forget about Mrs Reed malevolence and not become resentful.

Chapter 7

The winter is harsh and both the pupils and teachers suffer from the cold. Mr Brocklehurst comes to Lowood with his wealthy family, all wearing nice and warm clothes to lecture everyone on how important it is to be tough, humble and patient.

Jane cannot hide that she is bewildered by the narrow-minded and ridicule speech Mr Blocklehurst has just given, and seeing that, the man humiliates the little girl by repeating what Mrs Reed had previously said. Jane's hope for a bright future are suddenly darkened.

Chapter 8

Jane is desperate, but Helen and Miss Temple tell her that Mr Brocklehurst's speeches are usually not very popular. The director invite Jane and Helen for tea. Later, she writes a letter to Mr Loyd in favor of Jane, to make sure her reputation is safe.

Chapter 9

At springtime, the boarding house is struck down by an epidemy of typhus fever. The insalubrity and poor hygiene conditions are endemic to the boarding house.
Many pupils get very ill, and some die. Jane meets a new friend named Mary Ann Wilson, but regrets Helen's absence who is sick and dying. Jane manages to see her one last time and falls asleep by her side. The following day, Helen dies.

Chapter 10

Because of the terrible epidemy, Mr Brocklehurst is compelled to improve the life conditions in his boarding house. Jane remains in Lowood for eight years, and teaches for two years there. Following Miss Temple's wedding and departure, Jane finally leaves Lowood. After some time considering wether she should or not publish an ad to be private tutor, Jane finally makes up her mind. She receives a letter from a certain Mrs Fairfax who lives in Thornfield-Hall. Bessie, who is a servant in Gateshead comes to see Jane and tells her that a Mr Eyre came to the estate years ago when Jane was in Lowood. The man had to leave before he could get a chance to see her.

Chapter 11

Jane Eyre arrives in Thornfield-Hall where she meets with Mrs. Fairfax. Mrs Fairfax is a widow. She becomes Adèle Varens' private tutor, who has just arrived from France with Sophie. Mr. Edward Rochester owns the estate but is hardly ever there. For the first time, Jane hears a rather strange and demoniac laughter from inside the house. Mrs Fairfax is reprimanding Grace Poole who is a servant at the estate.

Chapter 12

Jane finds felicity at Thornfield-Hall but still hears strange noises. She leaves Adèle recovering from a cold and goes to a post office that is two miles away. On her way, she meets with a stranger whose horse has just slipped on the road. She helps him getting back on his horse because he has sprained ankle. Once back in Thornfield-Hall, Jane understands that the stranger was in fact Mr Rochester.

Chapter 13

The castle is more and more lively. Mr Rochester invites Jane and Adèle to have tea with him and asks lots of question to Jane. He also wants to make sure she is competent. Jane gets to know a few things about her master's past.

Chapter 14

Mr Rochester is a social person. One night, he invites Jane and Adèle out. Adèle who is a little pretty damsel got a gift but Mr Rochester is a little tired of her twittering all the time. Curious about Jane, he speaks with her and seem to enjoy her personality. He also talks about Céline's mother for whom he has spent a lot of money.

Chapter 15

In this chapter, we get to know about Mr Rochester's former passion for an Opera ballet, named Céline Varens. He took care of her until he found out she was cheating on him.

She gave birth to a little girl and declared that Mr Rochester was the father. She run away with her lover to Italy, leaving her little girl behind. Mr Rochester chose to keep the little girl with him. Later, a strange laughter awoke Jane who saved Mr Rochester from a fire that had been lit in his room. The man is grateful and agrees with Jane who believes Grace Poole to be guilty.

Chapter 16

Mr Rochester has not told anyone about Jane's intervention. The composure that Grace Poole shows while she is guilty of a murder attempt leaves Jane disconcerted. Mr Rochester goes with Mr Eshton to join an aristocrat club for a few days. When Jane hears that Miss Blanche Ingram might marry Mr Rochester, she realizes how her social status is lower than Mr Rochester's.

Chapter 17

Mr Rochester has been away for two weeks when he announces that he will be back within three days with a few guests, including Miss Ingram. Jane and Adèle do not take part of the celebrations. The following day, Mr Rochester invites them to join him in the living room. Though Miss

Ingram does not appear to be such a nice person, it seems that her charms do work on Mr Rochester. Seeing this, Jane prefers to run away.

Chapter 18

Mr Rochester's guests occupy themselves with various activities, including riddles. Miss Ingram and Mr Rochester do not really seem to be attracted to each other. Jane learns that this marriage is nothing else than a marriage of convenance. Mr Mason, a stranger, arrives while Mr Rochester is absent. The arrival of a Bohemian who pretends she can see in the future is expected. The girls (including Jane) are encouraged to hear about their future and it appears that Miss Ingram is quite upset with what she has just been told.

Chapter 19

Jane is the last one to join the Bohemian in the small room to hear about her future. She gets to know that Mr Rochester and Miss Ingram's wedding might be cancelled. The Bohemian starts doing a portrait of Jane before telling her about her real identity: The Bohemian happens to be Mr Rochester in disguise, which upsets Jane a lot. The news that Mr Mason has come to visit upsets Mr Rochester. Jane assures Mr Rochester of her support.

Chapter 20

The castle is awaken by a terrifying scream, and a great confusion follows. Mr Rochester pretends that it was a fragile servant and asks Jane for help. She has to take care of Mr Mason while Mr Rochester goes to fetch the doctor. Jane is puzzled and wonders about the situation. After her master returns, she understands that the guest has been stabbed and assaulted by the demoniac laughing woman. Mr Rochester has Mr Mason leave with the doctor.

Chapter 21

Bessie's husband, Robert Leaven, comes to inform Jane that John Reed has died and that Mrs Reed is sick. Before she leaves to be with her aunt, Jane tells Mr Rochester that she has decided to find a place in another house and will leave after his marriage with Miss Ingram. In Gateshead, Jane sees Bessie, Eliza and finally Georgiana. She stays by Mrs Reed bedside who keeps talking down on her. Jane decides to stay for a few days and socialize with her cousins. Mrs Reed gives Jane a letter from John Eyre, her uncle who wished to adopt her, and dies the following night.

Chapter 22

After the funeral, while Georgiana is the first to leaves and join her family, Eliza chooses to go to a convent. As for Jane, she goes back to Thornfield-Hall. Much to her surprise, she finds Mr Rochester is still there. Despite the gloomy future that she expects, Jane is delighted to see the man she is falling for, and a little puzzled too by the absence of preparations for the marriage she resents.

Chapter 23

One night, Jane meets Mr Rochester in the garden. He promises her to find her a new position. And while Jane is devastated, Mr Rochester declares his love for her. He has never felt anything for Miss Ingram who was only interested in his money. Jane tells Mr Rochester that she loves him.

Chapter 24

Mr Rochester decides that he will marry Jane in four weeks. He informs Mrs Fairfax who is rather confused by her master's behabiour. The widow tells jane that their marriage will be seen as a misalliance because of their different social backgrounds. Jane has one condition for this marriage to happen though: she wants to keep her position.

Chapter 25

Jane keeps having nightmares about a vampire. These sound like an ill omen in regards to their love. Mr Rochester tries to soothe her.

Chapter 26

Though the marriage was planned to be private, it is prevented by Mr Briggs and Mr Mason who claim that Mr Rochester is already married. His first wife is apparently Mr Mason's sister: Rebecca Mason. Mr Rochester married this woman fifteen years eralier but was not aware of her madness. Back in the castle, Jane sees Rebecca Rochester who has turned out insane. Jane is again devastated by this terrible news and the fact that she can no longer trust the man she loves.

Chapter 27

Mr Rochester tells about how his first marriage, which was a marriage of interest with painful and disastrous consequences. As he could not get a divorce, he had to support Adèle's mother. Meeting Jane looked like the possibility to make amends. Jane refuses to be his mistress and decides to leave Thornfield-Hall, to her lover's utter despair.

Chapter 28

During three days, the young woman roams in the heath and has to beg for food at several times. Worn out and starving, she wants to find help in the Moor-House where Mary and her sister Diana live. Hanna, the servant refuses to welcome her and coldly rejects her.
She is finally saved by St John, Mary and Diana's brother, who takes her in. Both sisters offer their help.

Chapter 29

Jane remains sick for three days. The Rivers look after her and Hanna finally becomes milder. The two sisters have to teach to earn money, just like Jane. Back from a walk, St John wants to know who Jane is and why she is here. She tells him her story without telling too much about what really made her leave Thornfield-Hall. Finally, the Rivers family wants her to stay with them.

Chapter 30

The three young woman get along very well and Jane learns a lot with them. St John is too busy with preaching and is more distant and gloomy. The house will soon be empty because the sisters are leaving to teach and St john is going back to the presbytary in Morton with Hanna. St John asks Jane if she would like to work there. She learns that their uncle died and that he has ruined their father, leaving them nothing to the benefit of another heir.

Chapter 31

Jane lives in a little abode in Morton where she has twenty pupils. St John visits her. He intends to become a missionary and will soon leave for India. Jane meets Miss Rosamond Oliver who is a young rich girl with great physical and moral assets. She discovers that St john is sensible to her charms.

Chapter 32

Jane is a successful teacher. Miss Oliver's advances have no effect on St john. The man is resolved to sacrifice everything for his professional decision. Eventhough Mr Oliver does not have anything against a marriage between his daughter and St john, the young man refuses and believes that Miss Oliver would never be a good missionary. He then leaves hastily.

Chapter 33

The young man comes back the following day to announce to Jane that she is his cousin. They have the same uncle, John Eyre who used to live in Madera and died recently. He left all his money to Jane who is suddenly very rich and happy to find out she does have a family. In the following days, Jane will do everything she can to have her cousins back to Moor-

House. The three girls won't have to work again and Jane will give a small amount of money to her other cousins.

Chapter 34

Before Christmas, Jane can finally leave her position as a tutor. She gets Moor-House ready before her cousins' arrival. We learn that Miss Oliver will marry a certain Mr Granby. The young woman focus on the projects that are dear to them and to make her cousin happy, Jane learns hindu. He finally proposes her but after thinking about it for a while, she declines it. St John is really upset and their relationships will now be cold.

Chapter 35

Even though St Jones is implacable, jane tries to make up with him. The departure of her brother is a sad thing for Diana, who rejoices that Jane does not go with him. Before his stay in Cambridge, St John proposes again to Jane who finally changes her mind. The following night, the woman hears Mr Rochester's voice. She desperately tries to find out where he is, but with no luck.

Chapter 36

St John left for Cambridge, and before he did, he told his bride to be to be wise and humble. Jane leaves for Thornfield-Hall where she finds that the estate has turned into a ruin. She learns that Rebecca Rochester has set fire to the place, and destroyed it. Mr Rochester has greatly suffered from Jane's departure, he has turned blind after the fire and is now very lonely. He lives in the Ferndean manor, a family property, with two servants, named John and Mary.

Chapter 37

Jane gets to the manor just before dawn. She arrives while Mr Rochester is taking a walk. She introduces herself to Mary and convinces her to let her join Mr Rochester in the living room. When he sees her, he seems to be getting back to life. After long passionnate talks, he proposes her again and Jane accepts with no hesitation.

Chapter 38

The wedding happens in the most private manner, with not even a witness. The Rivers sisters are enthusiastic for her cousin. Adèle goes to a school that is nearer to the estate and ten years later, the love Jane and Rochester share is still passionate. Mr Rochester recovered his sight two years after the marriage and gave Jane a child. Mary and Diane Rivers also got married and both live a happy life. St John, on the other side, is still a bachelor and lives in the Indies.

REASONS
OF SUCCESS

Read.

Queen Victoria has ruled over Great Britan since 1837. She succeeded in imposing herself though her predecesors have had troubled and questionable reigns. Ireland, which was part of the British Empire, demanded its independency and was responsible for a series of bombing that the Queen had to deal with.

The Victorian era was mainly marked by discipline and morals. In order to fix the mistakes of her predecessors, whose reigns were marked by scandals of all sorts, the Queen opted for a rigorous and strict policy on religion and morals.

A new social class which was modelled after the Queen, was born: the bourgeoisie. Contrarily to the idle aristocracy, the bourgeoisie turned out to be a hard-working and pious class, dedicated to a radical and exacerbated form of protestantism called puritanism, including the cult of domesticity and marriage.

Moral and religious rigorism appeared and new principles were established, against the women's rights. Indeed, the British Bourgeoisie established an idealised status for women who had to be spiritual guides at home, but not assertive and independant strong women.

The only means for women to acquire a respectable social status was to get married, but they did not have any rights and were only the occasion for the family to get money from the husband once the marriage was set.

Working for a woman was not accepted as it was common and normal at the time that women were and had to be financially dependant. Most women who had to work were from the middle class and single, either because of their appearance or their poverty. Also, women can only work as nurses, teachers or servants and finding a position was very hard.

The novel as a literary genre has been despised for decades, and was considered to be shallow and lacking any interest. It attracted mostly a feminine audience, and from the XVIIIth century on, lots of women will start writing novels. As it was not considered a noble genre, it was not taken seriously and was seen as more accessible to women. Moreover, reading was considered as dangerous and compromising for women. As women wanted to preserve their private life and stay out of trouble, they tended to use male pseudonyms to make their way to the literary world. Novelists like Mary Roberts Rinehart or Mary Howitt supported their families thanks to their literary activities.

British realism was born at the end of the XVIIIth century, thanks to writers like Henry Fielding or Tobias Smollett, but it was officially recognized in the second half of the XIXth century. Mary Ann Evans, best known as Georges Eliot, wrote *Adam Bede*, *Romola*, *Middlemarch*. Elizabeth Gaskell also described various social classes in her novels. She first published anonymously and only later used her real name.

Mrs Gaskell was from the aristocracy and did not know much about more modet social classes. Her novels were thus closer to fictions and romances. She wrote *Mary Barton*, *Ruth* and *Wives and Daugthers*.

The romanesque and realism genres were also interesting for male writers. Some like Charles Dickens, with *Oliver Twist* or *Little Dorrit* gave an ideal vision of characters who embodied the fragile and pure woman. Others like Thackeray with *Vanity Fair* are more critical of the puritan society but very hypocrite at the same time. The most famous writers and also the most critical towards British society were Herbert Georges Wells, best known as H. G. Wells, Thomas Hardy, or Anthony Trollope

Charlotte Brontë started to write at a time when realism imposed itself as a logical sequel to romanticism.

She was influenced by romanticism and Jane Eyre does

contain romantic and gothic elements. Also, there is a first person narrator and the expression of feelings takes an important place along the novel. Before she went to the boarding school, Jane, who is the narrator, was living a very unhappy life. As a passionate woman, she ends up falling for her master, Mr Rochester, who appears to be as exalted as she is. He is described as the tyical byronic Hero: a libertine, original, excentric and passionate character.

In regards to the Gothic aspect of the novel, there are many surreal events which appear, reminding us of the Gothic novel. Moreover, a place like Thornfield-Hall's manor can only be reminiscent of the Gothic genre. The meetings and many of the events happen at dawn (clair de lune), giving a surreal and somehow magical touch to the novel.

Charlotte Brontë simultaneously approach more modern themes. The characters are meticulously described, both morally and physically. Contemporary subjects are dealt with too, like boarding schools for girls, or the very poor conditions in which servants had to live with like insalubrity, disease and such.

The author reminds of Elizabeth and Maria's deaths, which were the consequences of insalubrity in the boarding-schools at the time.

Her depiction of the puritan society is another aspect of realism in her novel. Mr Brocklehurst stands for the endemic hypocrisy of a society that wanted to look moral and right-minded. The Reed family, Mrs Ingram and her daughter Blanche embody the Aristocracy which despised the inferorio lower social classes.

Finally, Jane Eyre also seems to be morally right and rigorous. For instance, once she learns about his first marriage, she refuses to stay with Mr Rochester despite all the love she has for him. She chooses to run away from him and from her feelings. Then she refuses to marry St John because she wants a marriage of love, and not a marriage of interest.

After her first novel, *The Professor* had been rejected by the Smith, Elder and Co publishing house, Charlotte Brontë tried again with *Jane Eyre*. This time, it is a success. Elizabeth Gaskell was a great friend of Charlotte Brontë, and after her death, she wrote a biography entitled *The Life of Charlotte Brontë* that was published in 1857. The greeting *Jane Eyre* received when Jane Eyre got published is related in the biography:

"When the manuscript of Jane Eyre had been received by the future publishers of that remarkable novel, it fell to the share of a gentleman connected with the firm to read it first. He was so powerfully struck by the character of the tale, that he reported his impression in very strong terms to Mr. Smith, who appears to have been much amused by the admiration excited. 'You seem to have been so enchanted, that I do not know how to believe you,' he laughingly said. But when a second reader, in the person of a clear-headed Scotchman, not given to enthusiasm, had taken the MS. home in the evening, and became so deeply interested in it, as to sit up half the night to finish it, Mr. Smith's curiosity was sufficiently excited to prompt him to read it for himself; and great as were the praises which had been bestowed upon it, he found that they had not exceeded the truth."

In order to have more chances to get her novel edited, Charlotte Brontë chose to sign her novel with a male pseudonym, Currer Bell. Robert Southey, who was a romantic writer, would have deterred Charlotte from writing as it was seen as an immoral activity for women.

Nevertheless, thanks to the success of Jane Eyre, Anne and Charlotte will want to unveil their real identity, and will go to London to meet Mr Smith in person. He will be very surprised. There was a high chance that this revelation would shock society, no matter how successful was the novel. Also, the fact that the main character was a passionate, witty and independant women would be unbearable. Little by little, the Brontë sisters will be forgotten.

Since she was a little girl, Charlotte Brontë had always been an imaginative person. The Brontë children, who were most time alone, created an imaginary world where they felt safe and happy. They also had pleasure in writing stories and were encouraged to read very early.

Charlotte's father, Patrick Brontë used to read the Blackwood's Magazine. It was first named The Blacwood's Edinburgh Magazine though, and it was a british publication, from 1817 to 1980. It was founded by Wiliam Blackwood and its content was made of articles about romanticism and the gothic, which were two declining literary trends at the time. Wiliam Blackwood influenced many writers, especially the Brontë sisters, but Edgar Allan Poe too.

The Brontë children first discovered Lord Byron's character while reading this magazine. Lord Byron created the prototype of the Romantic hero who fought for the freedom of a people.

MAIN THEMES

The main theme of the novel which was a contemporary theme at the time, is feminine independence. It is progressively and through a series of stages that the narrator wins her independence.

The narrator was a baby when her uncle and aunt, Mr and Mrs Reed took her. The lack of care and general indifference she was vicitm of, made her an unhappy and solitary child who did all she could to avoid her cousin John who kept abusing her. She tried her best to be loved but with no success, and after a fainting fit, she got sent to a boarding school. This was a chance to escape from the estate where she grew up: "Ere I had finished this reply, my soul began to expand, to exult, with the strangest sense of freedom, of triumph, I ever felt. It seemed as if an invisible bond had burst, and that I had struggled out into unhoped-for liberty." (Chapitre 4).

This is when she first experienced freedom and independence.

After eight years in Lowood as a pupil and then a teacher, and as a result of Miss Temple's marriage and departure, the young girl wants to discover the outside world.

This sudden change in a life governed by a strict schedules and specific habits will overwhelm the girl who finds herself boundless and free to leave Lowood.

She still has to work for someone else as her modest life does not allow her to be socially recognized.

Jane Eyre realizes it by herself: "But women feel just as men feel; they need exercise for their faculties, and a field for their efforts, as much as their brothers do; they suffer from too rigid a restraint, too absolute a stagnation, precisely as men would suffer; and it is narrow-minded in their more privileged fellow-creatures to say that they ought to confine themselves to making puddings and knitting stockings, to playing on the piano and embroidering bags. It is thoughtless to condemn them, or laugh at them, if they seek to do more or learn more than custom has pronounced necessary for their sex." (chap 12)

Nevertheless, being a servant at the time was highly despised, and a woman who dared to work and support her family was considered as disrispectful of the place she had been given. Mrs Ingram's position about this are very clear. As for Blanche Ingram, she believes servants are "a plague". These two arrogant, proud and tough women ignore that Jane Eyre is not bothered about what they think. Eventhough she is considered as inferior, the young woman noticed one thing: despite her fortune, her beauty and her culture, Blanche Ingram does not attract Mr Rochester, who will later confess to Jane that he only courted Miss Ingram to make her jealous.

When Jane Eyre returns to her family to see her dying aunt, she is very indifferent to her cousins' behaviour: "A sneer, however, whether covert or open, had now no longer that power over me it once possessed: as I sat between my cousins, I was surprised to find how easy I felt under the total neglect of the one and the semi-sarcastic attentions of the other--Eliza did not mortify, nor Georgiana ruffle me. The fact was, I had other things to think about; within the last few months feelings had been stirred in me so much more potent than any they could raise--pains and pleasures so much more acute and exquisite had been excited than any it was in their power to inflict or bestow--that their airs gave me no concern either for good or bad." (Chap 21). The once dying for love little girl grew up to become independent from a family who never had any love nor esteem for her.

When Mr Rochester wants to marry her, she accepts on one condition: she will still be able to work and remain independent, unlike Adèle's mother: "I only want an easy mind, sir; not crushed by crowded obligations.Do you remember what you said of Celine Varens?--of the diamonds, the cashmeres you gave her? I will not be your English Celine Varens. I shall continue to act as Adele's governess; by that I shall earn my board and lodging, and thirty pounds a year besides." (Chap 24)

While she is about to get married and financially safe, Jane Eyre still claims her indepence and her right to exist. Mr Rochester does not fail to mention it: "You entered the room with a look and air at once shy and independent." (Chap 27).

He also deplores Jane's decision to run away from him when she discovers that he is already married: "Never, 'said he, as he ground his teeth,' never was anything at once so frail and so indomitable." (Chap 27) Still, he does not try to hold her back and though he knows that everything now is over, he tries to convince her with words.

Later on, the reason why Jane refuses to marry her cousin St John, is her will to stay upright. She did not fail to see that the man did not love her but found that her honesty, humility and wisdom would make her a good missionary. This sounded sad for Jane who only dreamt of a loving marriage.

"Alas! If I join St. John, I abandon half myself" (Chap 34).

The cold, harsh and distant behaviour that St John has later, only comforts the woman's decision.

"I felt how--if I were his wife, this good man, pure as the deep sunless source, could soon kill me, without drawing from my veins a single drop of blood, or receiving on his own crystal conscience the faintest stain of crime" (Chap 35).

Later on, Jane is thrilled by the religious commitments and dedication of the young man and changes her mind.

When she first met Mr Rochester, Jane considered him as her master, and not because their love is shared means that things will deeply change. Indeed, Mr Rochester will organize everything. But the penultimate chapter stands as a final stage in the woman's quest for her own indentity. When she comes back to Mr Rochester, she tells him that she just inherited from an uncle:

"– No, sir! I am an independent woman now.

– Independent! What do you mean, Jane? [...]What, Janet! Are you an independent woman? A rich woman?

– [...] I told you I am independent, sir, as well as rich: I am my own mistress." (Chap 37)

Jane Eyre does not see Mr Rochester as her master anymore, but as a friend she wants to help. He finally becomes her husband. And she is now a rich woman who does not have to work anymore. She does not have to marry someone to have a comfortable life, and if she marries Mr Rochester, it is by choice and not because someone else told her to do so.

The heroine's quest for a marriage of love finally succeeds.

Three times, Jane sis being proposed. The first time, it was the man she loved and whol loved her, but marrying him would not be in accordance to her principles. The, she refuses a marriage of interest because she does not have any feelings for her cousin. She is a woman of integrity, no matter how painful this can be.

Having money is one aspect of freedom. This is why Jane works hard to get a living and not be needy. She only becomes fully independent when she inherits from her uncle.

ANALYSIS OF THE
LITERARY MOVEMENT

Major social, economical and technological changes (Industrial Revolution) took place under Queen Victoria's reign.

Realism as a literary genre was a logic trend at the time. It succeeded romanticism and all the passion, nostalgia and exoticism it bore. Conversely, realist writers tended to focus on society and its radical changes. They were more objective and used to describe and observe what happened around them in the most realistic manner. There was a specific description of both the intrigue and the character's feelings.

During the Victorian era, and as an echo to a conservative and idealist society, the novel staged characters who were concerned with their appearance and behaviour in a polished and righteous society.

Feminine characters are fragile and innocent and must be protected by a hero. In parrallel, writers are willing to describe a society they consider hypocrite, and especially in regards to the "fair sex".

The marriage market, for instance, which is a marriage of interest, of conveniences and not a love match, is especially criticized.

Realist authors also denounce all the social abuses which women have to endure. As people feel more and more concerned about feminism, writers tend to give to their female characters more and more space and importance. These feminine presence do matter, they are the heroine, and they do not depend on men anymore. Realism concentrates on marital and family relations, on social problems, and on profession. Writers are mostly interested in the differents social stratum: the bourgeoisie, the middle class and the working class.

Though "realist" writers come from various social backgrounds, they all had the opportunity at some time to read and to get an education. Their lifestyle was seen as scandalous at the time: they were single, and some were homosexual or even bisexual. They were not extrovert though and prefered to remain reserved. Women were more liberated but reserved too. These writers have a life that is away from the righteous ideals that are linked to marriage.